810L

PEACHTREE CITY
PLAN TO STAY™

PEACHTREE CITY LIBRARY
201 Willowbend Road
Peachtree City, GA 30269-1623
Phone: 770-631-2520
Fax: 770-631-2522

Fact Finders®

Biographies

Oscar De La Hoya

The Golden Boy

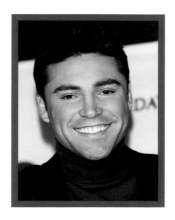

by Jeff Savage

Consultant:
Alex "The Bronx Bomber" Ramos
Founder, Retired Boxers Foundation, Inc.
Simi Valley, California

Capstone *press*®

Mankato, Minnesota

Fact Finders is published by Capstone Press,
151 Good Counsel Drive, P.O. Box 669, Mankato, Minnesota 56002.
www.capstonepress.com

Library of Congress Cataloging-in-Publication Data
Savage, Jeff, 1961–
    Oscar De La Hoya : the golden boy / by Jeff Savage.
    p. cm.—(Fact finders. Biographies. Great Hispanics)
    Includes bibliographical references and index.
    ISBN-13: 978-0-7368-6418-3 (hardcover)
    ISBN-10: 0-7368-6418-0 (hardcover)
    1. De la Hoya, Oscar, 1973– —Juvenile literature. 2. Boxers (Sports)—United States—
Biography—Juvenile literature. I. Title. II. Series.
GV1132.D37S39 2007
796.83092—dc22   2006003305

Summary: An introduction to the life of Oscar De La Hoya, the Mexican American boxer
    who rose from a life of poverty to become a world-famous athlete.

Editorial Credits
John Bliss and Jennifer Murtoff (Navta Associates), editors; Juliette Peters, set designer; Jan
    Calek (Navta Associates), book designer; Wanda Winch, photo researcher/photo editor

Photo Credits
Getty Images Inc./AFP/John Gurzinski, 5, 8, 25 (right); Getty Images Inc./Alexander
Sibaja, 26; Getty Images Inc./Allsport/Al Bello, 9; Getty Images Inc./Allsport/David
Cannon, 14; Getty Images Inc./Allsport/Holly Stein, 17 (inset); Getty Images Inc./
Allsport/Jamie Squire, 21; Getty Images Inc./Allsport/Jed Jacobsohn, 25 (left); Getty
Images Inc./Allsport/Mike Powell, 13, 15 (left); Getty Images Inc./Andrew D. Bernstein,
17, 27; Getty Images Inc./Holly Stein, 15 (right), 19; Getty Images Inc./ImageDirect/Evan
Agostini, 1; Getty Images Inc./Liaison Agency/Jeff Katz, cover, 22 ; Getty Images Inc./
Mike Powell, 11; Getty Images Inc./Robert Mora, 23; Los Angeles Public Library/Herald
Examiner Collection, 7; Zuma Press/Rob DeLorenzo, 18

1 2 3 4 5 6 11 10 09 08 07 06

Table of Contents

Chapter 1

New Champion

Oscar De La Hoya threw a fierce left jab and then a straight right. The punches cut Julio Cesar Chavez above his eye. Blood streamed down his face. De La Hoya delivered more punishing blows. Chavez was helpless against De La Hoya's lightning-quick hands. The crowd in Las Vegas, Nevada, was on its feet.

Outside of the ring, De La Hoya was a quiet gentleman. Inside the ring, he was a warrior. He was an Olympic star with 21 professional victories. Chavez was a Mexican legend in his 100th fight. He had lost just once. Chavez was a hero to De La Hoya.

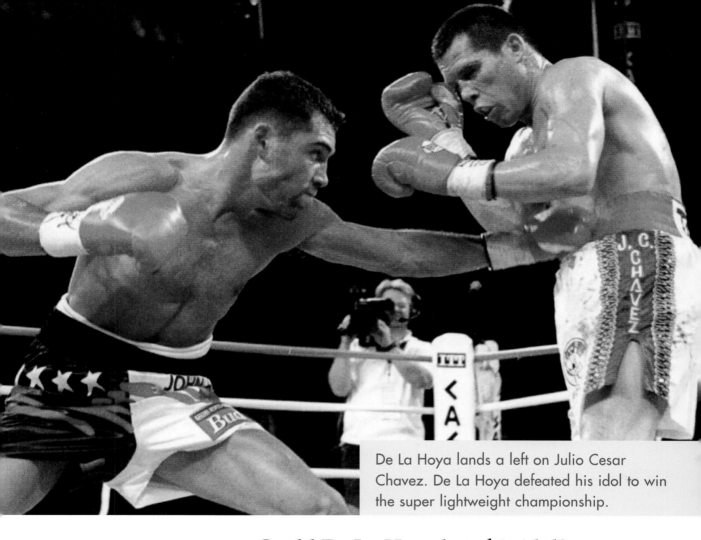

De La Hoya lands a left on Julio Cesar Chavez. De La Hoya defeated his idol to win the super lightweight championship.

Could De La Hoya beat his idol? Could he win this 1996 title fight? The fans watched as De La Hoya dodged punches. Suddenly, he unleashed a flurry of blows. The referee jumped in to stop the fight. De La Hoya had won. He raised his arms and flashed his electric smile.

Chapter 2

Childhood

Oscar De La Hoya grew up poor. He was born February 4, 1973, in East Los Angeles, California. His parents had moved there from Mexico.

De La Hoya's father, Joel, was a clerk at an appliance company. His mother, Cecilia, stayed home to take care of him, his older brother, Joel Jr., and his younger sister, Ceci. De La Hoya was often sent to the store. He bought groceries with food stamps. Food stamps are given to poor families so they can buy food. De La Hoya was embarrassed to pay with food stamps.

In 1979, when De La Hoya was 6 years old, Whittier Boulevard in East Los Angeles looked like this.

De La Hoya jabs and moves during a training session. He began to learn these skills at the age of 6.

Learning the Ropes

The family lived in a **barrio** with many street gangs. De La Hoya was picked on and beaten up. He grew tired of losing fights. At age 6, De La Hoya went with his father to a neighborhood gym to learn to box. His father and grandfather had been **amateur** boxers.

De La Hoya enjoyed the sport from the start. Wearing borrowed boxing gloves and shoes that were too big, he learned to jab, move, and defend himself. The neighborhood bullying soon stopped.

QUOTE

"Boxing is in my blood. From the day I put on the gloves, it's what I wanted to do."
—Oscar De La Hoya

When De La Hoya was 11, he watched boxing at the 1984 Olympic Games in Los Angeles. American boxer Paul Gonzales won a gold medal. De La Hoya liked the excitement. He decided then that he wanted to be an Olympic boxer. He found professional **trainer** Robert Alcazar and got started.

Robert Alcazar (right) helped De La Hoya train for the Olympics. ▼

Early Competition

De La Hoya was often asked to join street gangs. But at Garfield High School, he avoided the tough boys. He developed an interest in drawing and did well in **drafting** and art classes.

At age 15, he entered the famed Golden Gloves boxing tournament. He knocked out several opponents. Later that year, he became the Junior Olympic champion in the 119-pound weight class.

At age 16, he competed in the Goodwill Games. He won the gold medal at 125 pounds.

QUOTE

"I've been asked to join gangs, but I've never wanted to."
—Oscar De La Hoya

◄ De La Hoya posed for this publicity photo in 1990. By this time, he had already won several junior tournaments.

Chapter 3

Driven to Win

After winning the Goodwill Games in 1990, De La Hoya learned that his mother was seriously ill. He knew she had **cancer**. But her condition was getting worse. De La Hoya's family did not tell him until the competition was over. Cecilia De La Hoya told her son that she wanted him to win an Olympic gold medal. He promised her he would. She died that same year.

De La Hoya was driven to keep his promise. He ran at dawn, often around the cemetery where his mother was buried. De La Hoya fought every month. With each fight, he got better. In 1991, he won the amateur lightweight national title. He refused to lose.

De La Hoya trained hard for the Olympic Games. He had promised his mother before she died that he would win a gold medal.

De La Hoya hadn't lost a fight in four years. His next fight was the world championships in Sydney, Australia. Suddenly De La Hoya's winning streak stopped. He lost to Marco Rudolph of Germany. De La Hoya realized that he could be beaten.

The Games

De La Hoya made the Olympic team. He traveled to Barcelona, Spain, for the 1992 Summer Olympic Games. His dream was in sight. He beat opponents from Brazil, Nigeria, and Bulgaria to reach the semifinal round. The gold medal was nearly in his hands. Against Sung Sik Hong of South Korea, De La Hoya was knocked to the canvas. He got up just in time. De La Hoya managed to score a narrow win.

At the 1992 Olympics, De La Hoya won against Sung Sik Hong of South Korea in the semifinals. ▼

In the finals, De La Hoya defeated Marco Rudolph (in red).

De La Hoya proudly displays his Olympic gold medal. ▼

De La Hoya had reached the finals. His opponent was Marco Rudolph, the boxer who had beaten him in Sydney. The first two rounds were very close. In the third and final round, De La Hoya's face grew stern. He bombed Rudolph with punches and won the biggest fight of his life. He returned home from Spain and laid the gold medal on his mother's grave.

QUOTE

"I won this gold medal for my mom. Now the championship will be for me."
—Oscar De La Hoya

Chapter 4

The Golden Boy

De La Hoya was the only American boxer to win a gold medal in 1992. Sportswriters nicknamed him "the Golden Boy." He had an amateur record of 223–5, with 153 knockouts. De La Hoya decided to turn pro. Now he could earn money for his fights.

In De La Hoya's first professional match in 1994, he knocked down opponent Lamar Williams three times in the first round to win by a knockout. He earned $200,000 for the victory. Growing up, De La Hoya had little money, even for food. Now he could buy whatever he wanted. He bought a new four-bedroom house for his family. He also bought several new skateboards for himself.

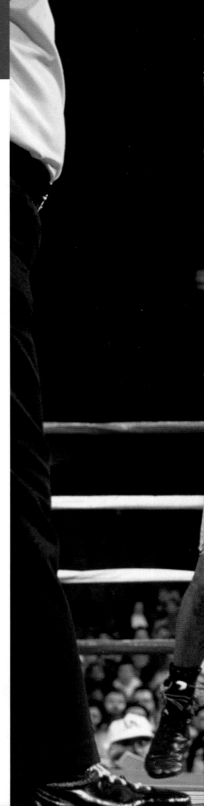

Before defeating Lamar Williams in his first professional match, De La Hoya showed his loyalties to both his Mexican and U.S. roots (inset).

De La Hoya won his first professional title, the junior lightweight, by defeating Jimmi Bredahl in 1994.

Capturing Titles

De La Hoya teamed with famous **promoter** Bob Arum, who arranged his fights. De La Hoya knocked out his next four opponents. In March 1994, he captured his first professional title by beating Jimmi Bredahl for the WBO junior lightweight title.

Later that year, De La Hoya entered the WBO lightweight class. He won the title with a knockout of veteran Jorge Paez. In May 1995, he pounded IBF champion Rafael Ruelas.

Finally, he faced and defeated Julio Cesar Chavez, "the old lion." De La Hoya was paid $9 million for the fight.

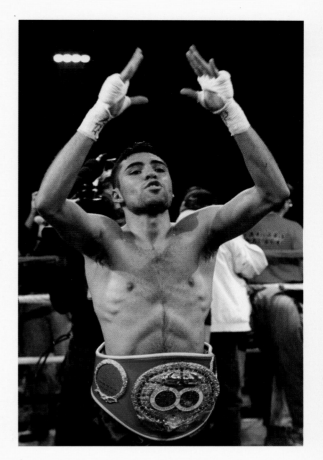

▲ After defeating Ruelas in 1995, De La Hoya blew kisses to the crowd.

FACT!

Major boxing organizations that award titles are the World Boxing Council (WBC), the World Boxing Association (WBA), the World Boxing Organization (WBO), and the International Boxing Federation (IBF).

Chapter 5

Mixed Reactions

De La Hoya was having great success in the ring, but some boxing fans were not impressed. His style was different from most boxers. He was not a brawler. He was polite and well mannered. He didn't have a bad attitude.

De La Hoya tried to outsmart his opponents. He jabbed and faked blows for a long time before throwing big punches. He rarely got hit.

Some Latino boxing fans felt that De La Hoya abandoned his community by moving to a mountain home high above Los Angeles. When he defeated Chavez in 1996, many Latinos in the crowd booed him. Chavez, not De La Hoya, was a hero to them.

De La Hoya's style drew mixed reactions from boxing fans. Here he enters Madison Square Garden for his fight with Derrell Coley in 2000.

Making Millions

Another thing that turned off some fans were De La Hoya's looks. He didn't look like a typical boxer. He didn't have scars or a broken nose. He didn't have tattoos. Instead, De La Hoya was handsome, with wide eyes and rosy cheeks.

These mixed reactions from boxing fans bothered De La Hoya. He knew how hard he had worked to become a champion.

◄ De La Hoya's good looks turned off some fans, who preferred boxers who looked tough.

Though fan disapproval bothered De La Hoya, businesses weren't bothered at all. They paid him millions of dollars to **endorse** products such as shoes, sporting goods, soft drinks, and shaving cream. He earned millions more from his fights. By 1997, De La Hoya was the third highest-paid athlete in the world. Growing up poor seemed so long ago.

QUOTE

"If I was scarred, if my nose was all busted up, they'd love me."
—Oscar De La Hoya

↟ Both his success at boxing and his good looks helped De La Hoya become very wealthy.

Chapter 6

Leaving His Mark

De La Hoya kept on winning. He beat many great boxers, such as Pernell Whitaker and Hector "Macho" Camacho. But De La Hoya was bound to lose one day. In 1999, he had his first loss as a pro to Felix Trinidad. A year later, De La Hoya lost to Sugar Shane Mosley. After a string of victories, he lost in 2003 to Mosley again. In 2004, he lost to Bernard Hopkins. De La Hoya had won world titles in six weight classes, but he was not invincible.

De La Hoya then took a break from boxing. But in May 2006, De La Hoya returned to the ring to face Ricardo Mayorga. He dominated the fight and won in the sixth round.

De La Hoya defeated Javier Castillejo to win his sixth WBC title. De La Hoya holds up fingers showing the number of WBC belts he has won.

"Outside the ring, I want no trouble with anybody. I want peace and tranquility. I want to be happy and enjoy life."
—Oscar De La Hoya

Success and Humility

Knowing that he can't box forever, De La Hoya started his own company called Golden Boy Enterprises in 1999. De La Hoya owns newspapers and office buildings in Los Angeles and New York.

In 2000, De La Hoya released an album of songs called *Oscar.* It featured the hit single *"Ven a mí."*

De La Hoya is a successful boxer, businessperson, and singer. But he remains humble. He carried a single food stamp in his wallet for fifteen years until his wallet was stolen. The stamp reminded him of how his hard work lifted him from poverty.

▲ De La Hoya and his wife Millie Corretjer attend the Annual Evening of Champions Awards in 2004. The couple was married in 2001.

Fast Facts

Full name: Oscar De La Hoya

Birth: February 4, 1973

Parents: Joel and Cecilia De La Hoya

Siblings: Joel Jr., Ceci

Hometown: East Los Angeles, California

Wife: Millie Corretjer

Children: Jacob, Devon, Atiana Cecilia, Oscar Gabriel

Education: Garfield High School in Los Angeles, California

Achievements:

Won Golden Gloves championship, 1989

Won Goodwill Games gold medal, 1990

Won Olympic gold medal, 1992

Won world title in six weight classes

Recorded album *Oscar* for EMI/ Latin Records, 2000

Time Line

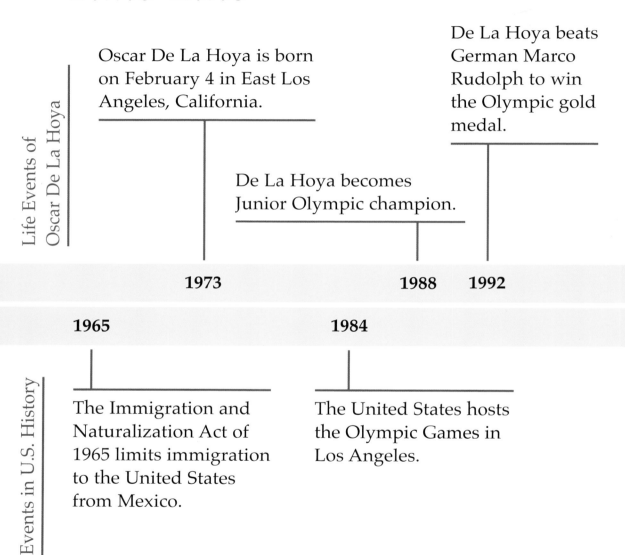

Life Events of Oscar De La Hoya

Oscar De La Hoya is born on February 4 in East Los Angeles, California.

De La Hoya becomes Junior Olympic champion.

De La Hoya beats German Marco Rudolph to win the Olympic gold medal.

1973   1988   1992

1965   1984

Events in U.S. History

The Immigration and Naturalization Act of 1965 limits immigration to the United States from Mexico.

The United States hosts the Olympic Games in Los Angeles.

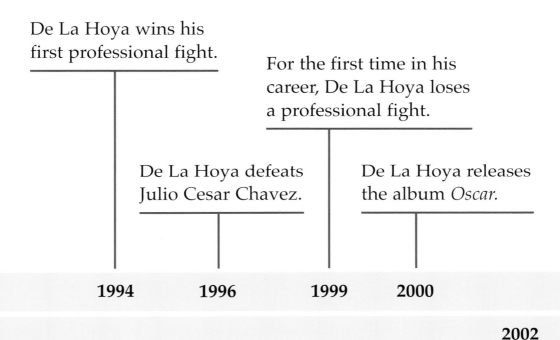

De La Hoya wins his first professional fight.

For the first time in his career, De La Hoya loses a professional fight.

De La Hoya defeats Julio Cesar Chavez.

De La Hoya releases the album *Oscar*.

1994 1996 1999 2000

2002

The U.S. Census Bureau determines that Hispanics have become the largest minority in the United States.

Glossary

amateur (AM-uh-chur)—someone who takes part in a sport or other activity for pleasure rather than for money

barrio (BA-ree-oh)—a neighborhood where Spanish is the main language

cancer (KAN-sur)—a serious disease in which some cells in the body grow faster than normal cells

endorse (en-DORSS)—to promote a product; celebrities are often paid for their endorsements of products.

drafting (DRAFT-ing)—a form of drawing that shows the construction of buildings and mechanical objects

promoter (pruh-MOH-tur)—a person who arranges boxing matches and creates interest in them

trainer (TRAY-nur)—a person who helps athletes get in the best condition to compete in a sports event

Internet Sites

FactHound offers a safe, fun way to find Internet sites related to this book. All of the sites on FactHound have been researched by our staff.

Here's how:

1. Visit *www.facthound.com*

2. Choose your grade level.

3. Type in this book ID **0736864180** for age-appropriate sites. You may also browse subjects by clicking on letters, or by clicking on pictures and words.

4. Click on the **Fetch It** button.

FactHound will fetch the best sites for you!

Read More

Kirkpatrick, Rob. *Oscar De La Hoya: Gold-Medal Boxer.* Reading Power. New York: PowerKids Press, 2000.

Quinn, Rob. *Oscar De La Hoya.* Latinos in the Limelight. Philadelphia: Chelsea House, 2001.

Shulman, Mark. *Super Oscar/Oscar De La Hoya.* New York: Simon & Schuster Books for Young Readers, 2006.

Index